TIME FOR KIDS

Earthquakes!

Cy Armour

Consultant

Timothy Rasinski, Ph.D.
Kent State University

Publishing Credits

Dona Herweck Rice, *Editor-in-Chief*
Robin Erickson, *Production Director*
Lee Aucoin, *Creative Director*
Conni Medina, M.A.Ed., *Editorial Director*
Jamey Acosta, *Editor*
Stephanie Reid, *Photo Editor*
Rachelle Cracchiolo, M.S.Ed., *Publisher*

Based on writing from *TIME For Kids*.

Teacher Created Materials

5301 Oceanus Drive
Huntington Beach, CA 92649-1030
http://www.tcmpub.com

ISBN 978-1-4333-3613-3

© 2012 Teacher Created Materials, Inc.

Table of Contents

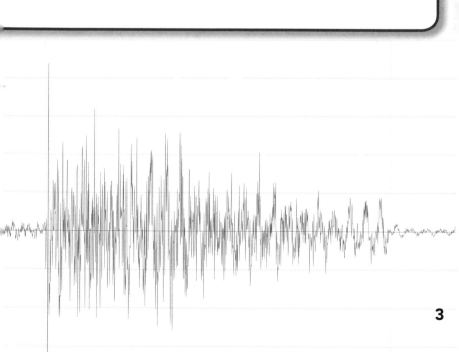

Earthquake!

Imagine you are sitting at the table, eating your cereal. Suddenly, the milk in the bowl starts to shake. The table begins to move. The ground beneath your feet is shaking.

What is happening?

It's an **earthquake!**

What should you do? Take cover! Get under the table. Crouch next to a sturdy object. Stay away from windows. Most of all, stay calm. You will be all right.

How Earthquakes Happen

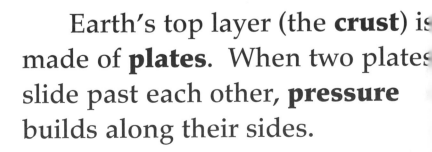

Earth's top layer (the **crust**) is made of **plates**. When two plates slide past each other, **pressure** builds along their sides.

fault line

This is land that has been cracked along a fault line.

When the pressure becomes too much, it is released. Then an earthquake happens.

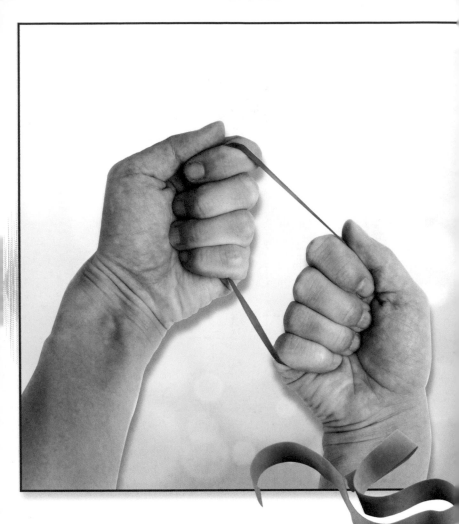

Think of it like a rubber band. Imagine you stretch the band more and more. Finally, it breaks. Snap!

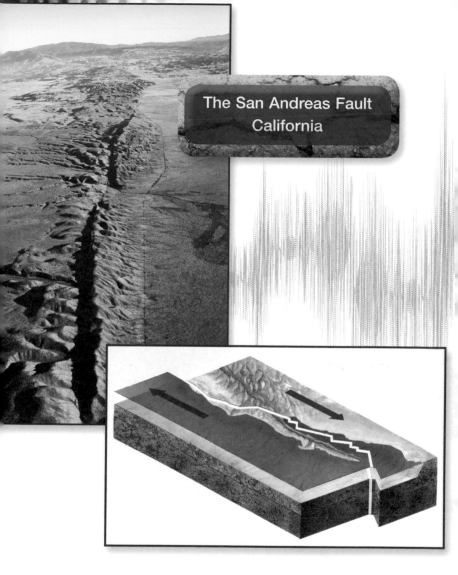

The San Andreas Fault
California

That is how an earthquake happens. The pressure builds, and then—snap!

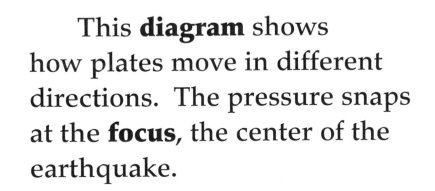

This **diagram** shows how plates move in different directions. The pressure snaps at the **focus**, the center of the earthquake.

The epicenter is the point on land above the focus of an earthquake.

picenter

focus

What Happens Next?

Once the pressure snaps, things start to shake. The shaking moves away from the focus across the land.

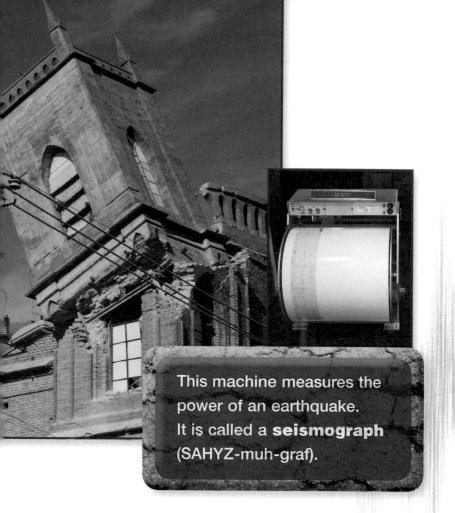

This machine measures the power of an earthquake. It is called a **seismograph** (SAHYZ-muh-graf).

On land, you can see the ground move. Buildings move and shake, too. If the earthquake is strong enough, buildings can fall down.

When an earthquake begins under the ocean, it makes the water move. There is a lot of water in the ocean! If all that water starts moving, it can make some big waves.

These big waves are called **tsunamis**. They are much taller and more powerful than other waves. They can cause a lot of damage.

A tsunami (soo-NAH-mee) used to be called a tidal wave. It is a very large and powerful wave that is caused by an earthquake.

Tsunamis can sink boats, tear down docks, and even destroy nearby buildings.

Earthquakes can happen anywhere. But they usually happen in certain places.

The west coasts of North and South America have many earthquakes. So does the east

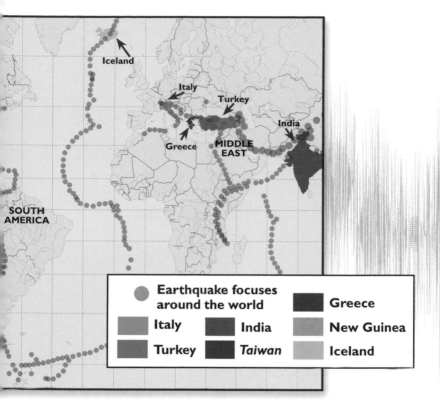

Earthquake focuses around the world

- Greece
- Italy
- India
- New Guinea
- Turkey
- Taiwan
- Iceland

coast of Asia. Italy, Turkey, Greece, India, and the Middle East have them, too.

Some of the most famous earthquakes have happened in these places.

San Francisco in California
had terrible earthquakes in 1906
and 1989. Both caused great
damage.

Japan and Haiti have had
many powerful earthquakes in
the last few years. Thousands
of people have died, and many
buildings have been destroyed.

But these earthquakes are rare. Most earthquakes are mild with little shaking.

Most of the time everybody is all right and things are fine.

Earthquakes are normal events on Earth.

Glossary

crust—the top layer of the earth

diagram—a drawing that shows how something works

earthquake—the shaking of the earth caused by plate movement and the release of pressure

focus—the center of an earthquake

plates—sections of Earth's crust

pressure—a great force

seismograph—a machine that measures the power of an earthquake

tsunamis—very tall and powerful waves caused by an earthquake